Notes

Published by
VINCENZO SGUERA
Via Provinciale , 68
24022 Alzano Lombardo
Bergamo (Italy)
Phone: (0039) 035515851
e-mail:
info@vincenzosguera.com

ARKIVIA
Books for Style

TECHNICAL DETAILS

THE CD ● The Book contains **2 FREE CD**.

TYPE ● The files contained in the **CD 1** are all **VECTOR** :
OF FILES this means in the first place that they can be
opened by all softwares that use **VECTOR** design.
It is made up of exact lines that delimit areas
where the colour is uniform.
This enables the design to be brought to any size
while retaining the maximum quality required.

● The files contained in the **CD 2** are all **BITMAP** .

SOFTWARE ● The main **VECTOR** softwares are :
ILLUSTRATOR (the first came out in1988),
CORELDRAW and **FREEHAND**.

● The **BITMAP** files (**FOLDER 4**) can be opened
in software such as **PHOTOSHOP**, **CORELPAINT**,
PAINTSHOP, **COREL PAINTER** etc..

SIZES ● The files are all real size 100%, that is, they
always match the **MODULE**, the part of
the texture which can be repeated to infinity
without discontinuity.

COLOURS ● The colours are in "**Four Colour Process Printing**",
that is **CMYK**.

● In **VECTOR** files the single colours are flat,
without transparencies or shading off.
By changing the **Four Colour percentages** they
can be modified within the software.

● Each single colour can be saved to prepare
films, calenders, looms.

● The colours used are at the most **8** , apart from
a few exceptions.
The background colour, even if white, has been
counted and also any colour which is repeated
in the design.

THE **FOLDERS** ● There are **4 FOLDERS** and each one contains the same **200 textures** but with different characteristics.

FOLDER 1 ● The designs have been created with **ILLUSTRATOR** in CD 1 so that a **CONTINUOUS PATTERN** can be edited from a **VECTOR** design.

● This sort of file, very useful for those who use **ILLUSTRATOR**, has been inserted in **FOLDER 1**.

● These files are in **AI** format

FOLDER 2 ● In **FOLDER 2** the "**ORIGIN**" files of the in CD 1 designs have been inserted: they also preserve the thicknesses, or rather the contours; both the colours and the size of these can be changed.

● All parts of the textures are always whole within the rectangle/module which acts as a cutting mask.

● These files are in **AI** format.

FOLDER 3 ● In **FOLDER 3** there are all the **MODULES**, in CD 1 with the same characteristics as **FOLDER 2**, but they are in **EPS VECTORIAL** format and every line has been changed into area.

FOLDER 4 ● At the end, for those who want to have in CD 2 **BITMAP** files in **EPS PHOTOSHOP** format, **300 dpi** and **CMYK**, they are in **FOLDER 4**.

All files can be opened by
● *ILLUSTRATOR 6* and following
● *CORELDRAW 8* and following
● *FREEHAND 8* and following
● *PHOTOSHOP* in any version

I think that it is possible to open these files with previous versions but I have not been able to verify this.

SOME EXAMPLES

You can use these textures on any kind of product simply filling in the shape and changing the colours as you wish.

tp0037

tp0014

tp0096

tp0061

tp0010

tp0040

tp0013

tp0175

tp0030

tp0098

tp0152

tp0018

tp0130

tp0005

tp0114

tp0084

tp0031

tp0145

SUMMARY
of TEXTURES

2 FLORAL POP

GEOMETRIC

FRESH

METRIC POP

These textures, typical of the fifties and sixties, with the advent of the computer, are becoming the right way to represent reality.

colors palette

tp0001 / pattern size: 18,00 cm x 20,00 cm

colors palette

colors palette

tp0002 / pattern size: 18,00 cm x 18,00 cm

pattern size: 27,00 cm x 27,00 cm / tp0003

colors palette

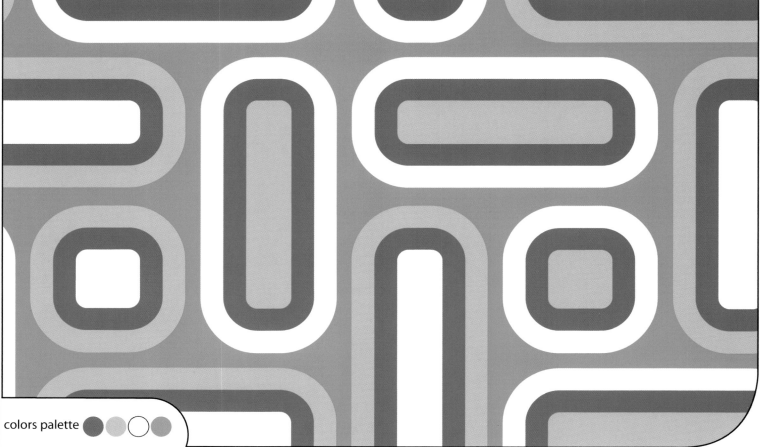

colors palette

tp0004 / pattern size: 24,00 cm x 24,00 cm

pattern size: 25,00 cm x 25,00 cm / tp0005

colors palette

colors palette

tp0006 / pattern size: 16,00 cm x 18,56 cm

pattern size: 7,30 cm x 7,30 cm / tp0007

colors palette

colors palette

tp0008 / pattern size: 21,00 cm x 16,00 cm

pattern size: 21,00 cm x 16,00 cm / tp0009

colors palette

pattern size: 25,00 cm x 18,00 cm / tp0010

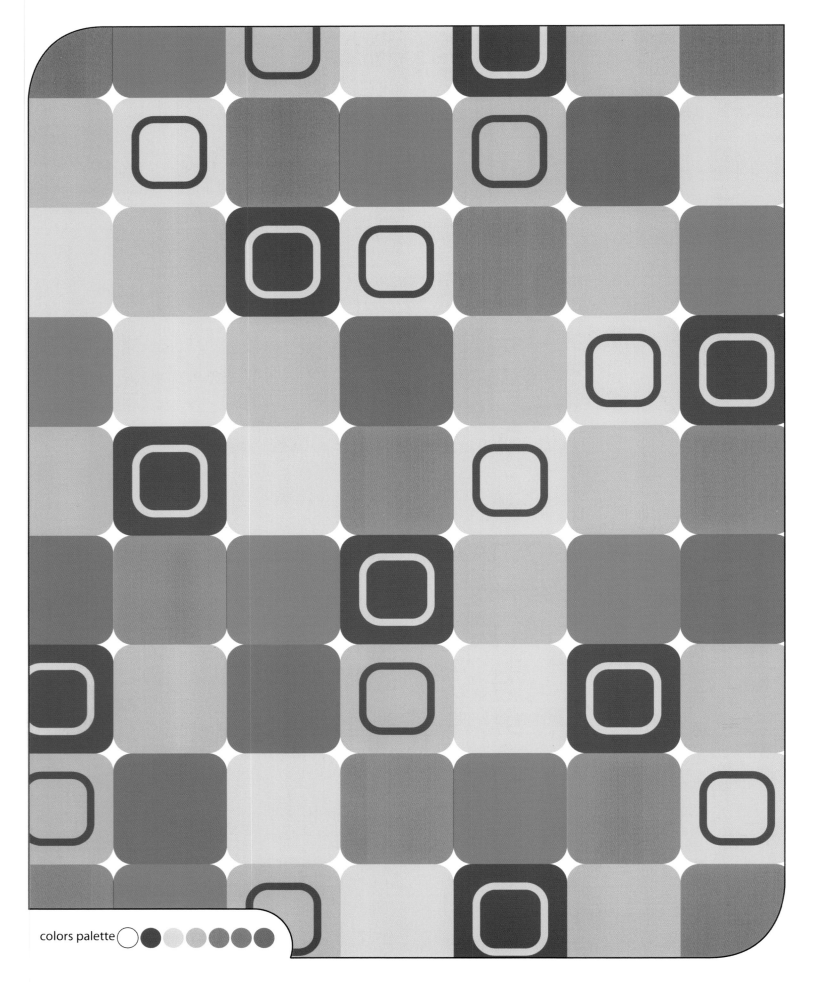

colors palette

tp0011 / pattern size: 24,00 cm x 24,00 cm

colors palette

pattern size: 32,00 cm x 24,00 cm / tp0012

colors palette ⚪🔘⚫

tp0013 / pattern size: 36,00 cm x 36,00 cm

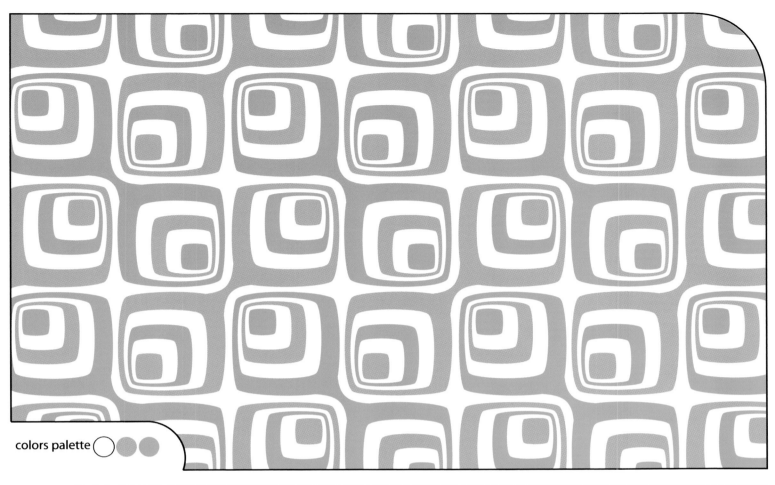

colors palette ○●●●

colors palette ●●●

tp0014 / pattern size: 30,00 cm x 30,00 cm

pattern size: 17,20 cm x 17,20 cm / **tp0015**

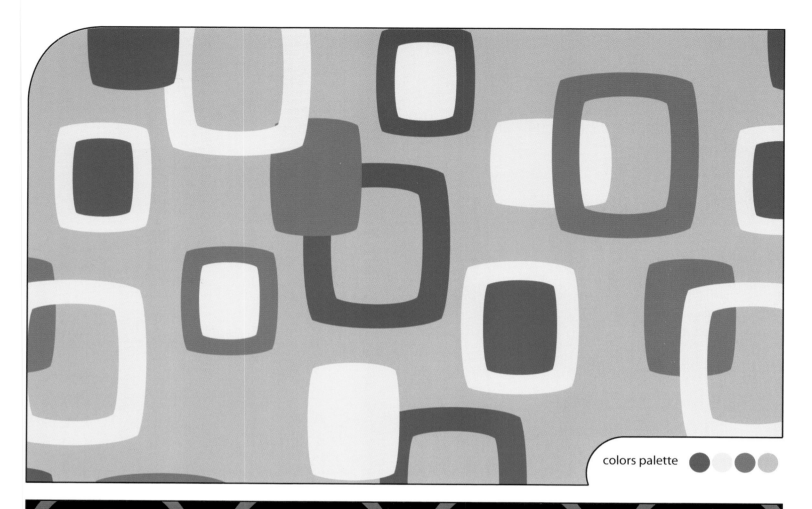

colors palette

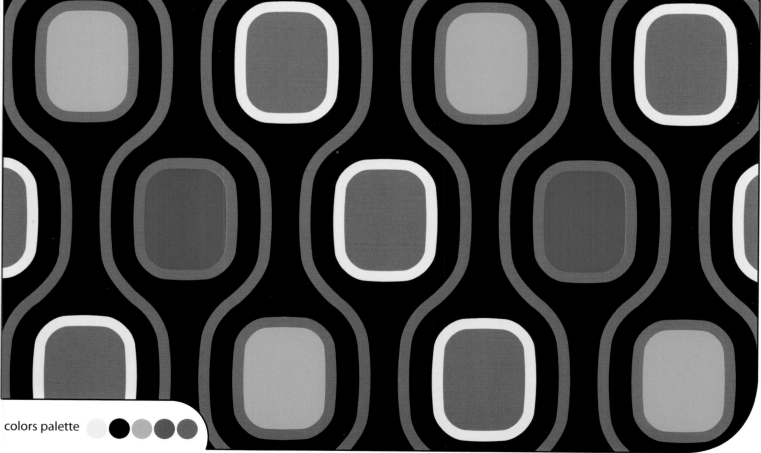

colors palette

tp0016 / pattern size: 18,00 cm x 24,00 cm

pattern size: 10,56 cm x 17,28 cm / **tp0017**

colors palette

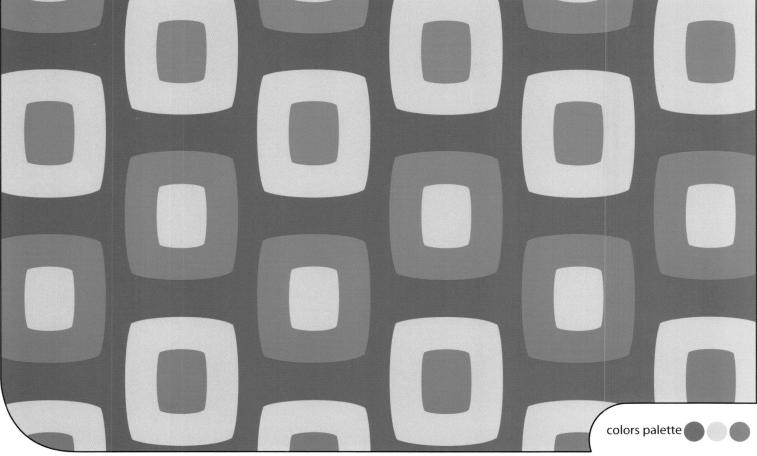

colors palette

tp0018 / pattern size: 30,00 cm x 30,00 cm

pattern size: 14,00 cm x 18,00 cm / tp0019

colors palette

colors palette

tp0020 / pattern size: 21,00 cm x 16,00 cm

pattern size: 16,80 cm x 16,80 cm / tp0021

colors palette

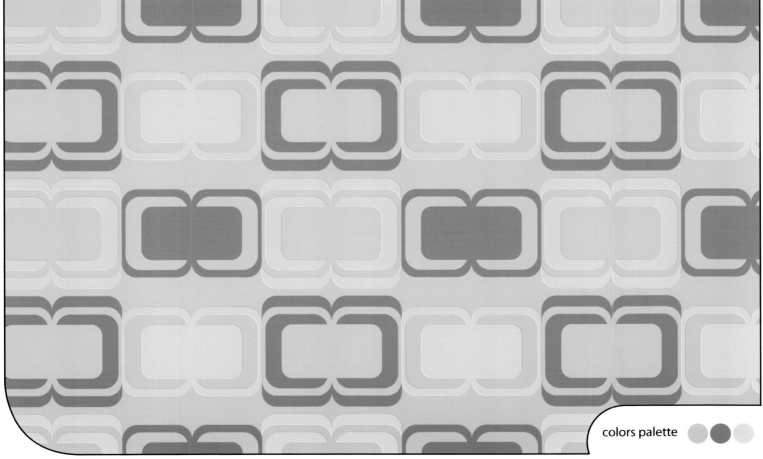

colors palette

colors palette

colors palette

tp0024 / pattern size: 25,00 cm x 25,00 cm

pattern size: 20,00 cm x 20,00 cm / tp0025

colors palette

colors palette

tp0026 / pattern size: 36,00 cm x 36,00 cm

Page
029

pattern size: 22,00 cm x 26,00 cm / tp0027

colors palette

colors palette

tp0028 / pattern size: 16,00 cm x 16,00 cm

pattern size: 20,40 cm x 20,40 cm / tp0029

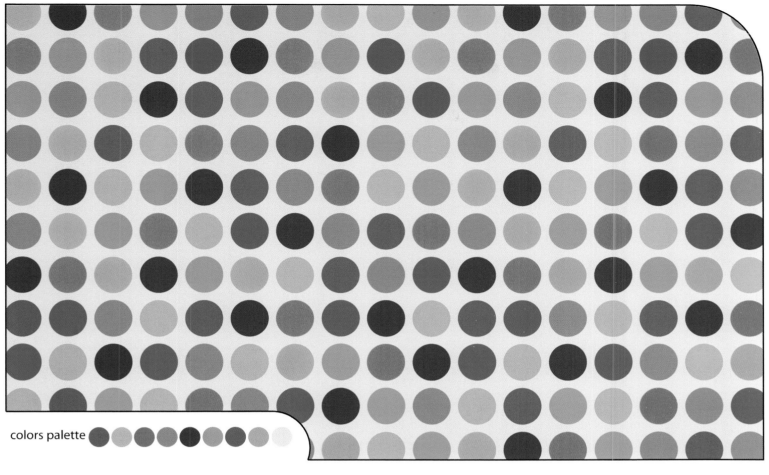

colors palette

colors palette

tp0030 / pattern size: 12,00 cm x 12,00 cm

pattern size: 10,40 cm x 10,40 cm / tp0031

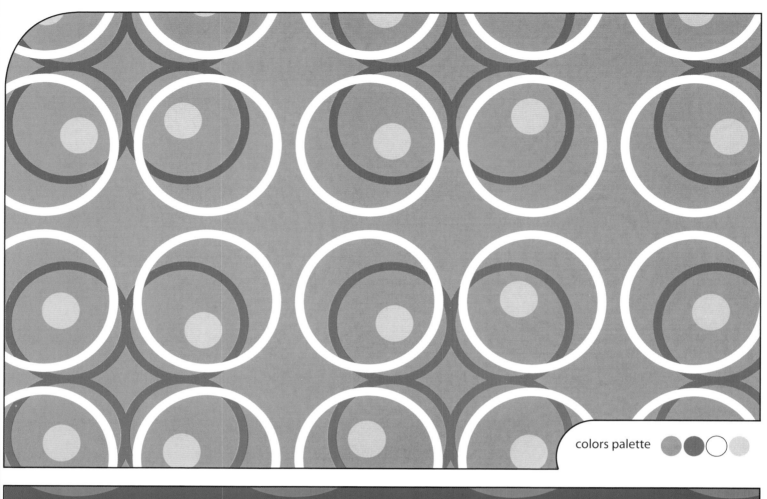

colors palette

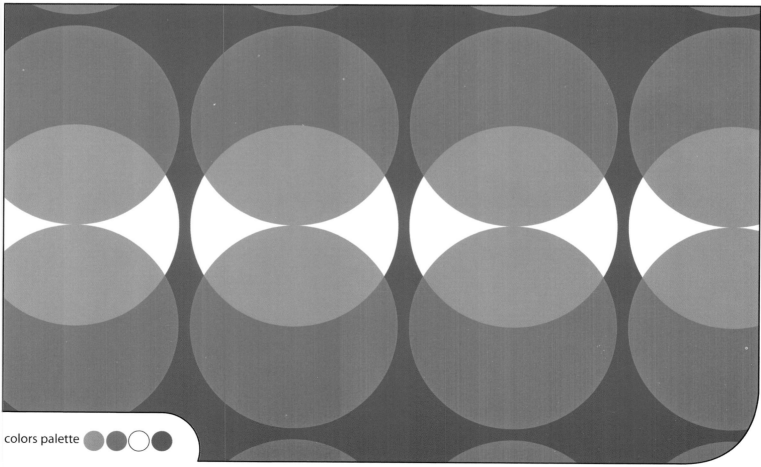

colors palette

tp0032 / pattern size: 17,20 cm x 17,20 cm

pattern size: 5,80 cm x 11,30 cm / tp0033

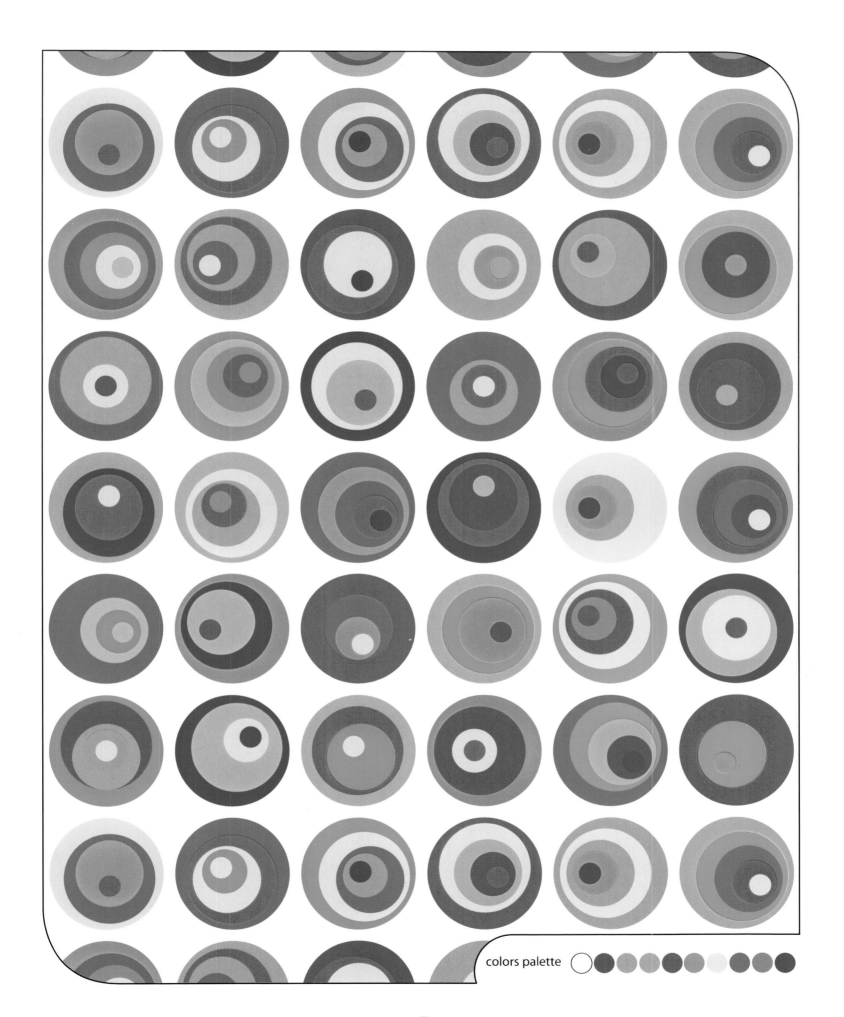

colors palette

pattern size: 20,00 cm x 20,00 cm / tp0034

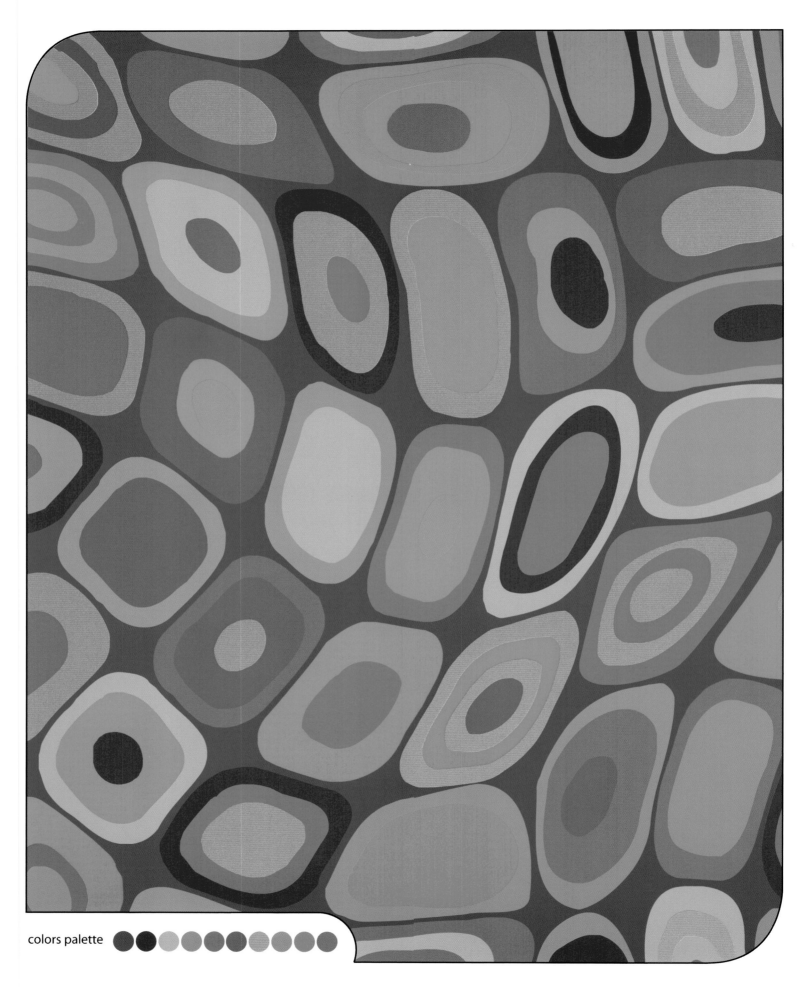

colors palette

tp0035 / pattern size: 23,66 cm x 26,65 cm

colors palette

pattern size: 26,00 cm x 26,00 cm / tp0036

colors palette

tp0037 / pattern size: 24,00 cm x 36,00 cm

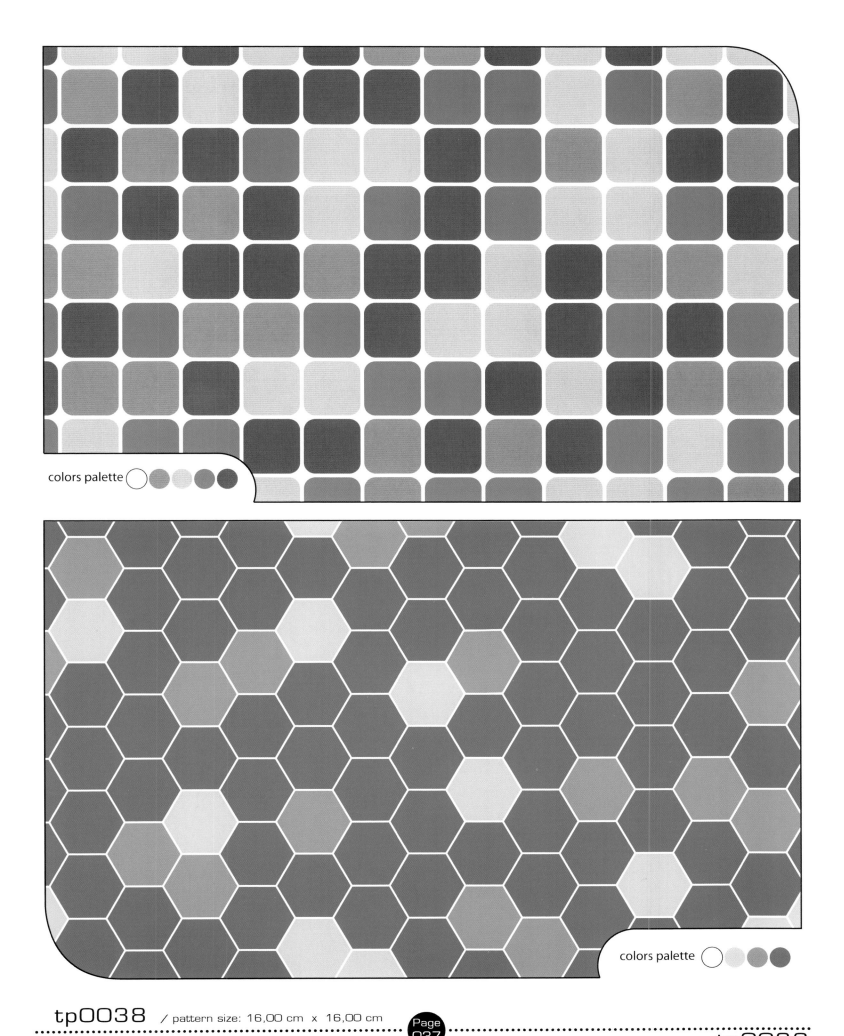

colors palette

colors palette

tp0038 / pattern size: 16,00 cm x 16,00 cm

pattern size: 21,00 cm x 29,50 cm / tp0039

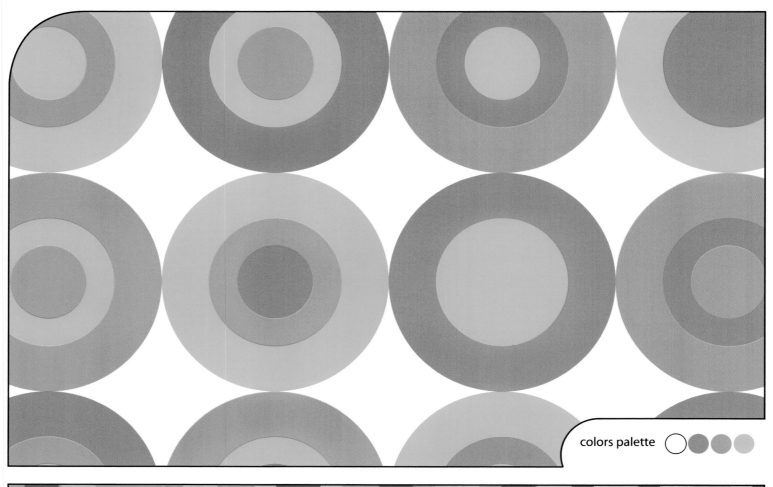

colors palette

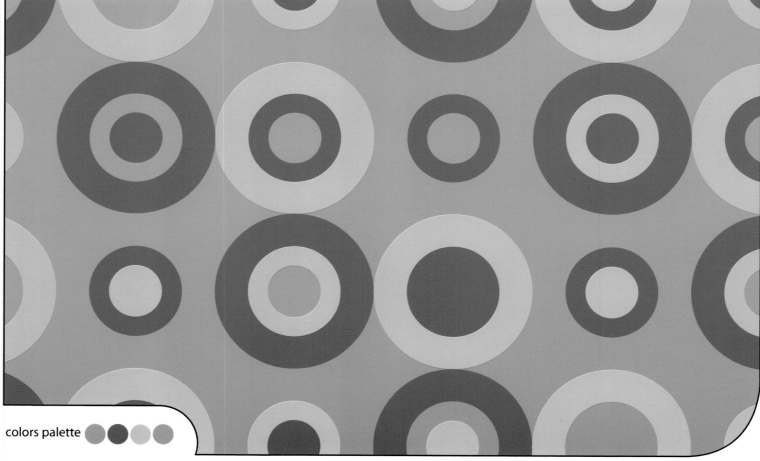

colors palette

tp0040 / pattern size: 36,00 cm x 36,00 cm

pattern size: 25,20 cm x 25,20 cm / tp0041

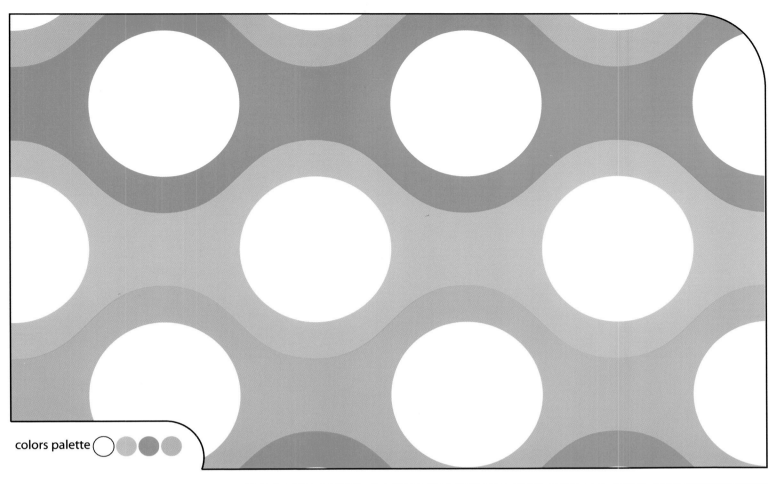

colors palette ⬤⬤⬤⬤

colors palette ⬤⬤⬤⬤

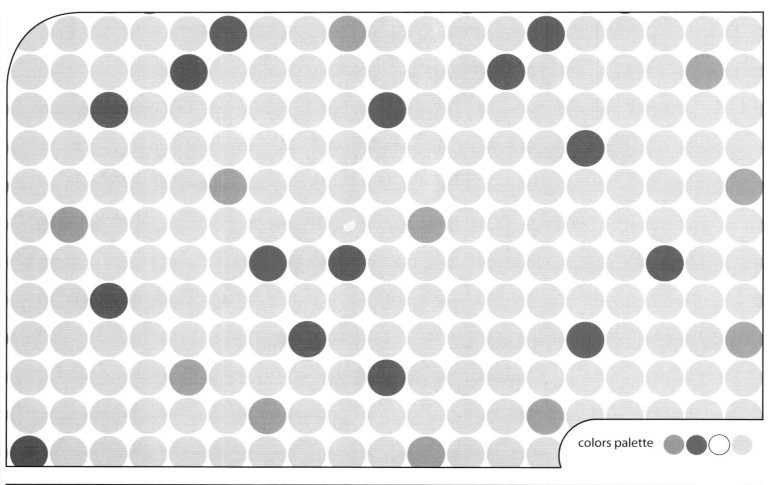

colors palette

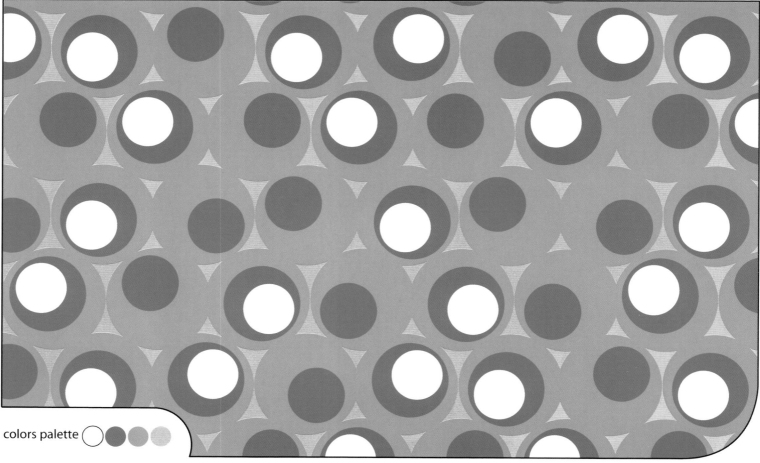

colors palette

tp0044 / pattern size: 19,95 cm x 27,30 cm

pattern size: 16,20 cm x 18,40 cm / tp0045

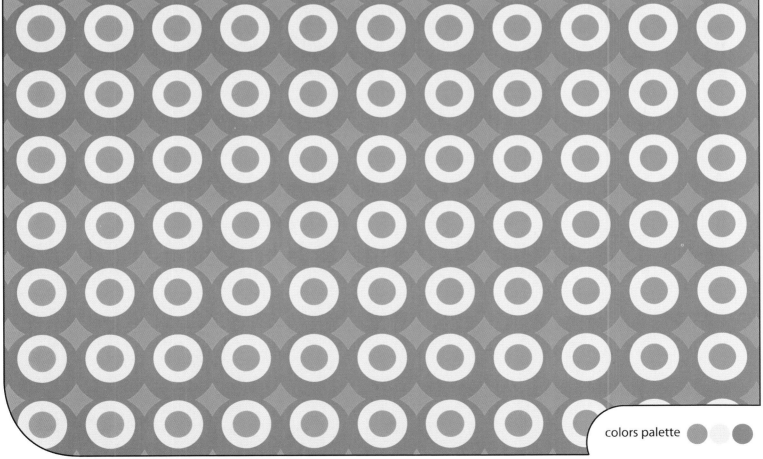

colors palette

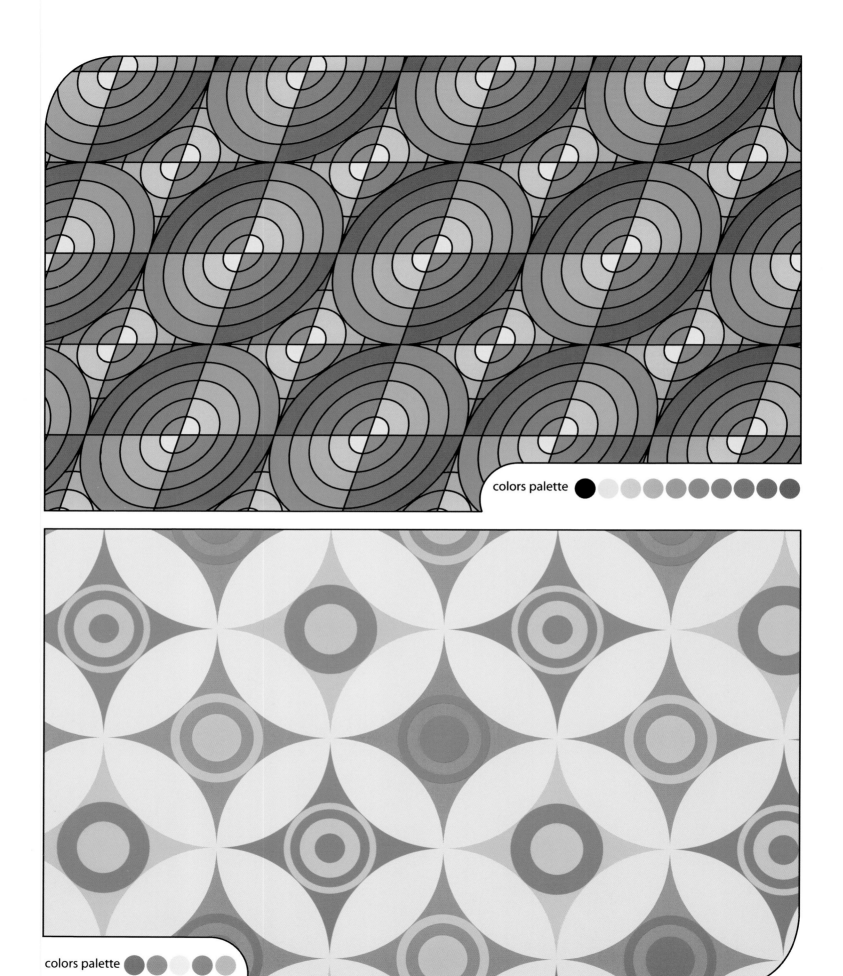

colors palette

colors palette

tp0048 / pattern size: 15,00 cm x 15,00 cm

pattern size: 12,00 cm x 12,00 cm / tp0049

colors palette

pattern size: 21,00 cm x 28,00 cm / tp0050

colors palette

tp0051 / pattern size: 24,00 cm x 24,00 cm

colors palette

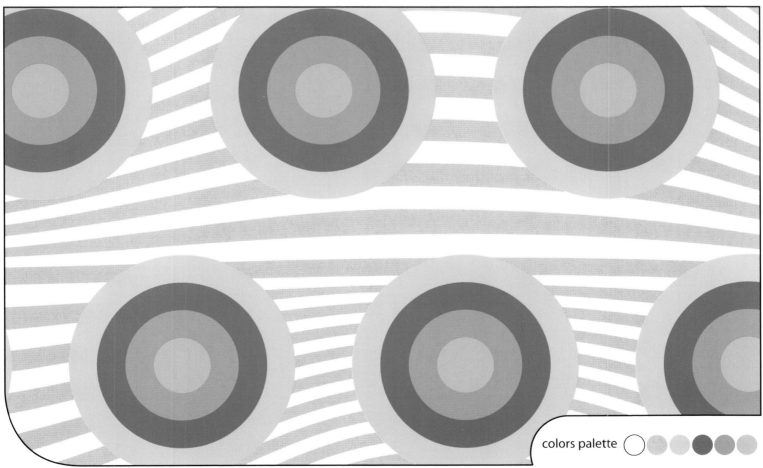

colors palette

colors palette

colors palette

tp0054 / pattern size: 25,00 cm x 35,00 cm

pattern size: 25,00 cm x 35,00 cm / tp0055

colors palette ⬤⬤⬤⬤

colors palette ⬤⬤⬤⬤⬤⬤

tp0056 / pattern size: 52,00 cm x 52,00 cm

pattern size: 17,50 cm x 67,50 cm / tp0057

colors palette

colors palette

tp0058 / pattern size: 6,00 cm x 4,40 cm

pattern size: 13,00 cm x 13,00 cm / tp0059

colors palette

colors palette

tp0060 / pattern size: 20,00 cm x 20,00 cm

pattern size: 24,00 cm x 24,00 cm / tp0061

colors palette ⬤⬤⬤⬤⬤⬤⬤⬤

tp0062 / pattern size: 30,00 cm x 30,00 cm

colors palette

colors palette

tp0063 / pattern size: 28,00 cm x 20,00 cm

pattern size: 25,00 cm x 28,00 cm / tp0064

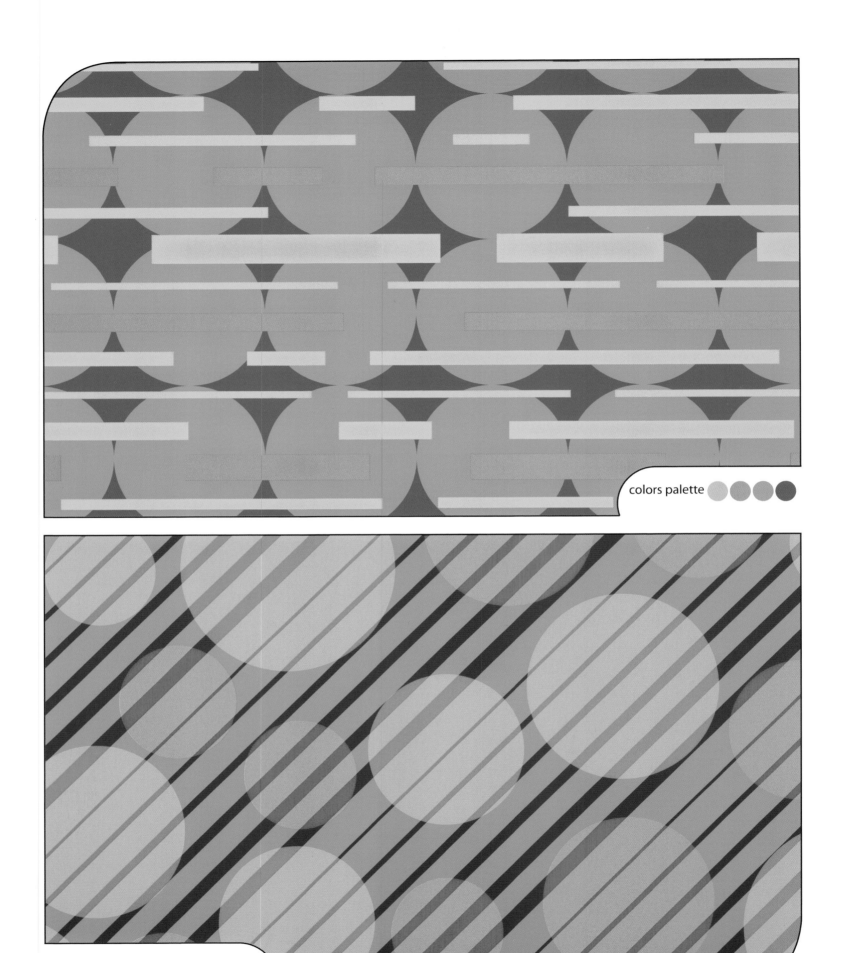

tp0065 / pattern size: 16,00 cm x 16,00 cm

colors palette

colors palette

pattern size: 31,20 cm x 15,60 cm / tp0066

colors palette

pattern size: 32,50 cm x 32,50 cm / tp0067

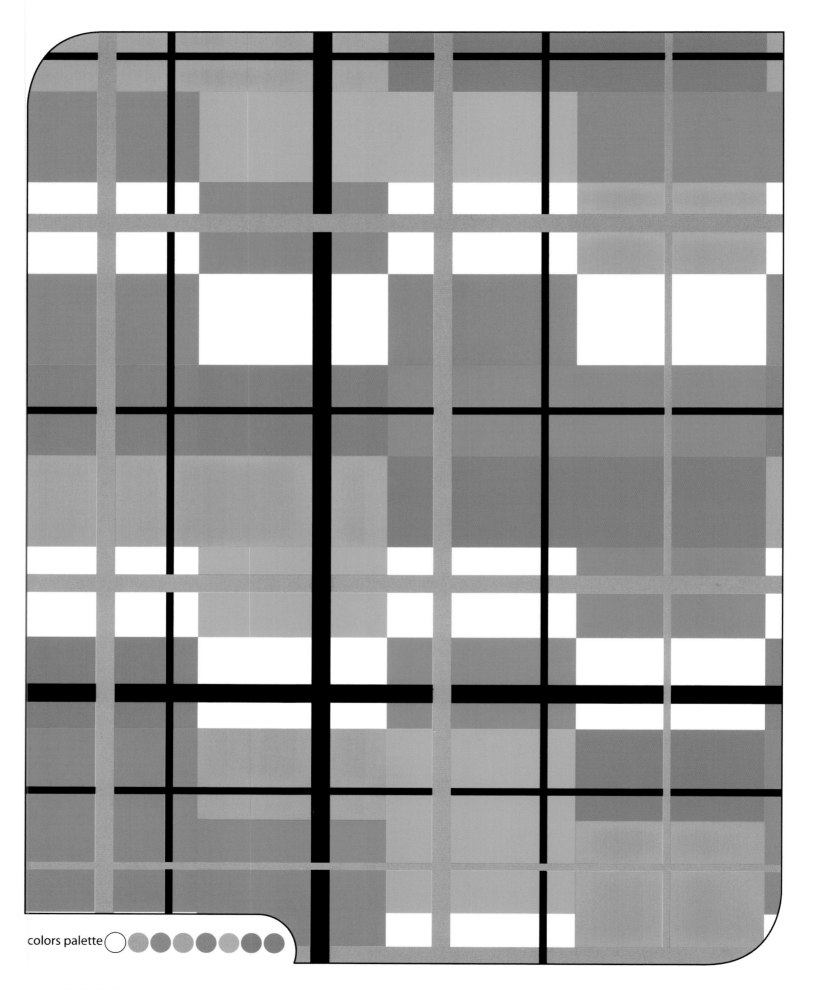

colors palette

tp0068 / pattern size: 20,00 cm x 40,00 cm

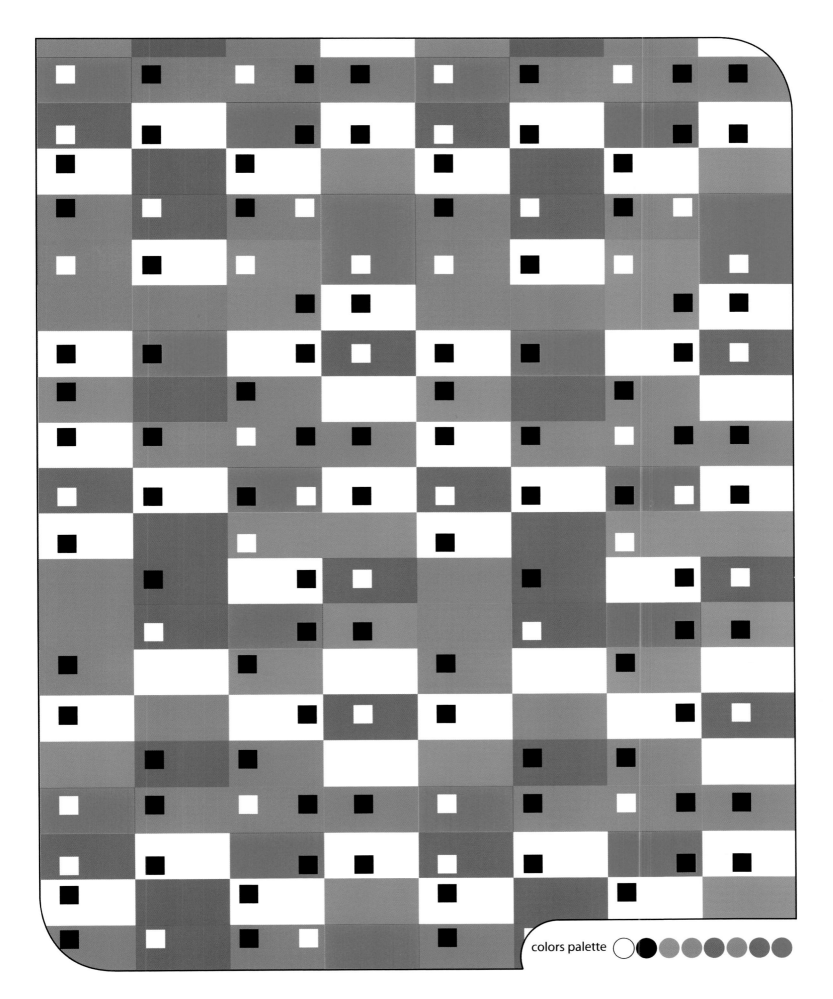

colors palette

pattern size: 10,00 cm x 20,00 cm / tp0069

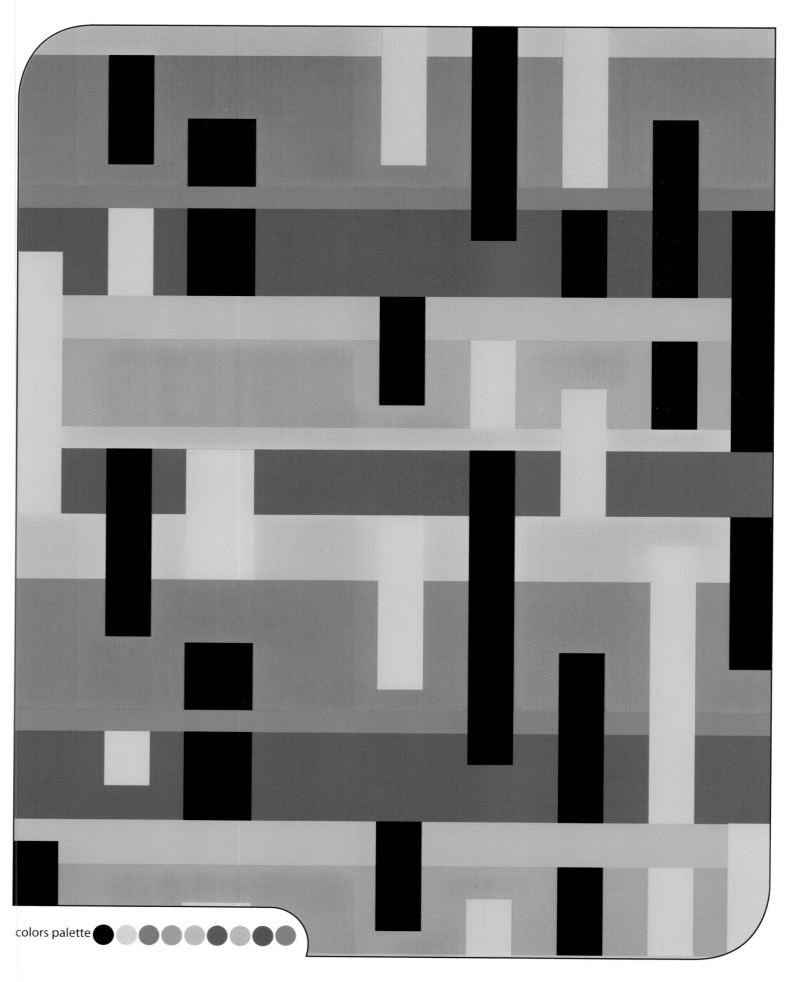

colors palette

tp0070 / pattern size: 43,20 cm x 28,80 cm

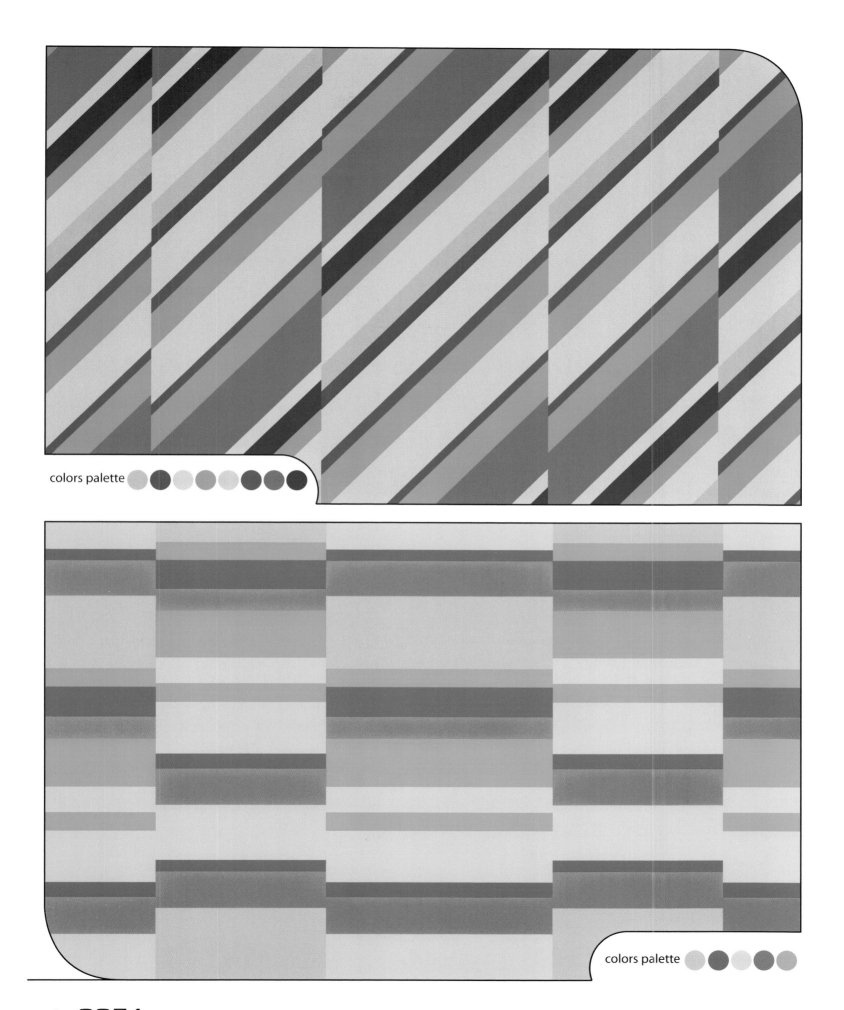

colors palette

colors palette

colors palette

colors palette

tp0073 / pattern size: 20,00 cm x 20,00 cm

pattern size: 21,00 cm x 12,75 cm / tp0074

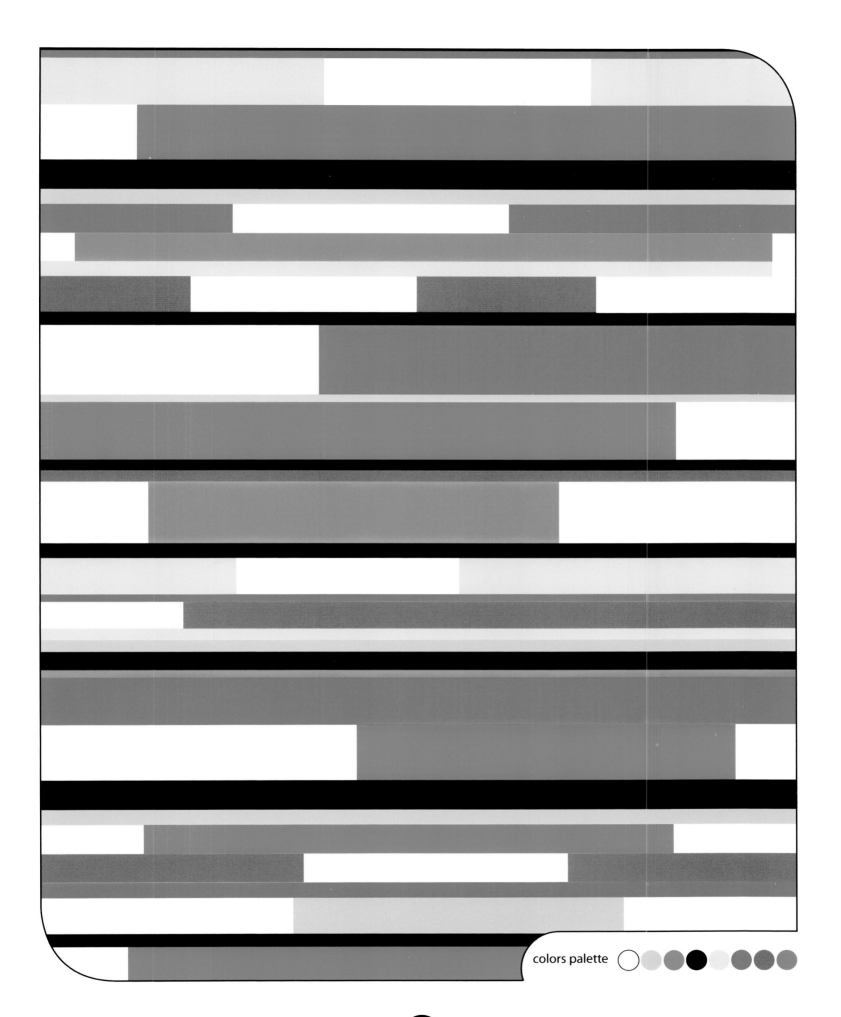

colors palette

pattern size: 44,00 cm x 34,00 cm / tp0075

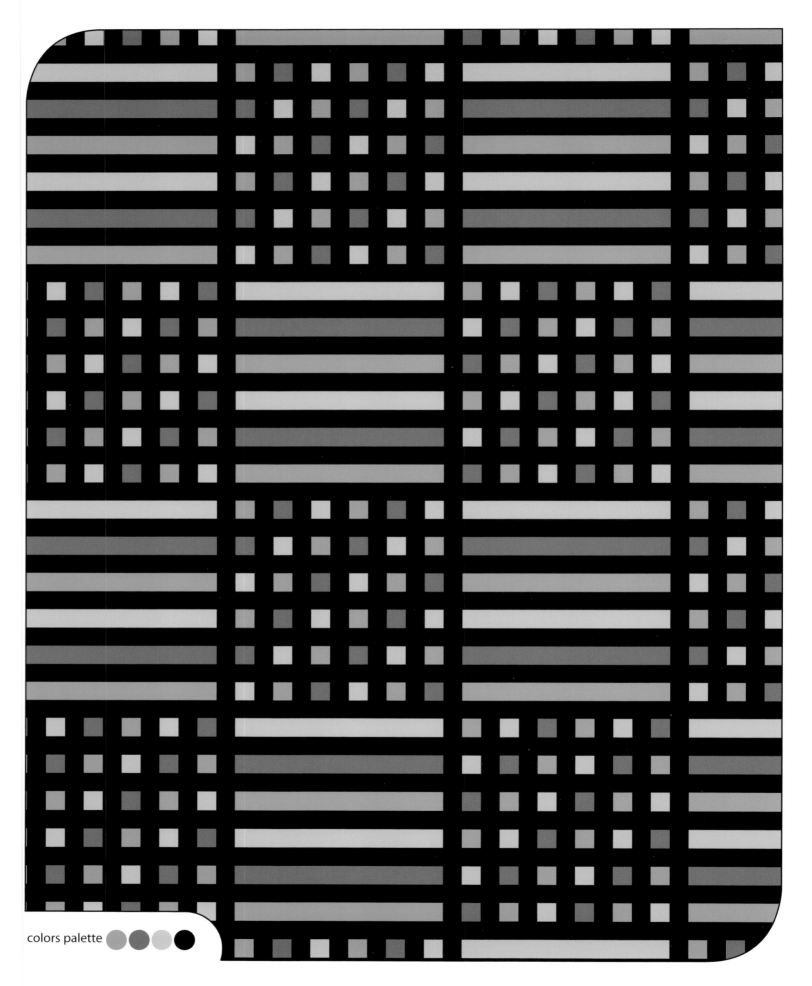

colors palette

tp0076 / pattern size: 24,00 cm x 24,00 cm

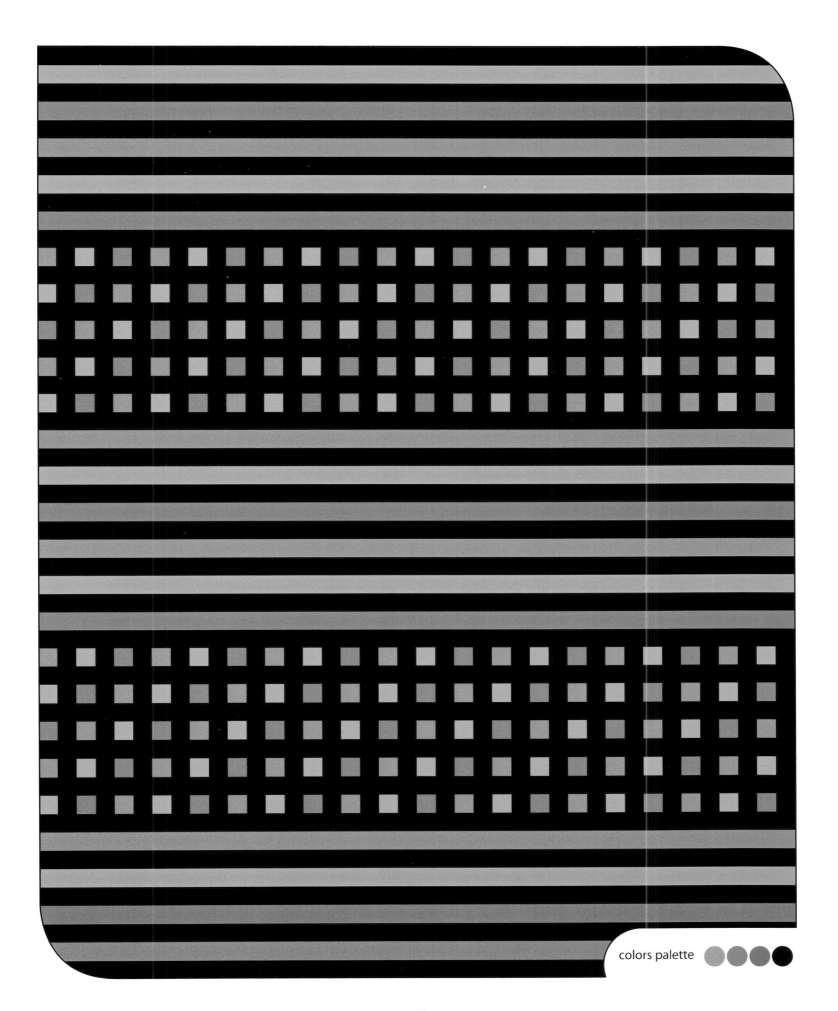

colors palette

pattern size: 21,00 cm x 22,00 cm / tp0077

colors palette

colors palette

colors palette

colors palette

colors palette

tp0081 / pattern size: 10,80 cm x 8,10 cm

pattern size: 28,00 cm x 20,00 cm / tp0082

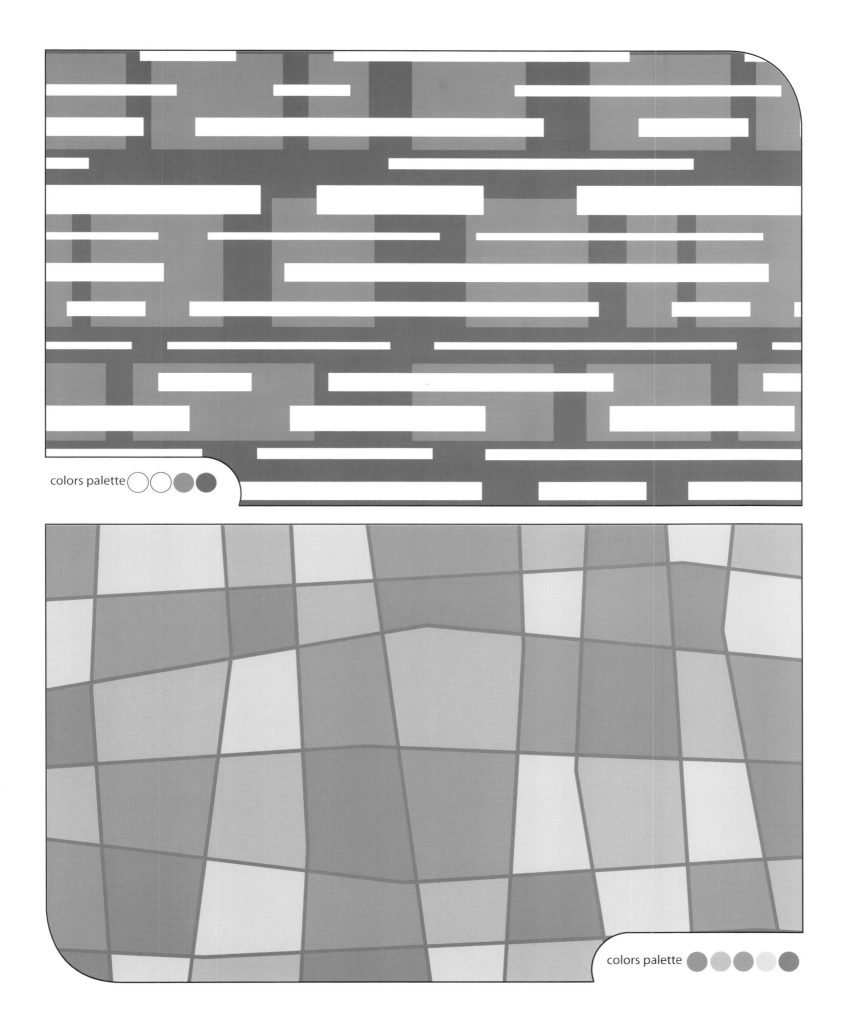

colors palette

colors palette

tp0083 / pattern size: 16,00 cm x 16,00 cm

pattern size: 280,00 cm x 28,00 cm / tp0084

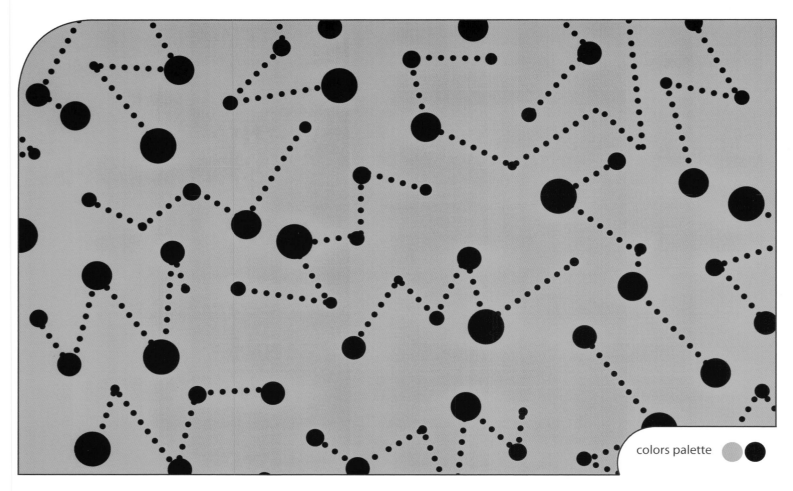

colors palette

colors palette

tp0085 / pattern size: 24,00 cm x 24,00 cm

pattern size: 27,30 cm x 39,00 cm / tp0086

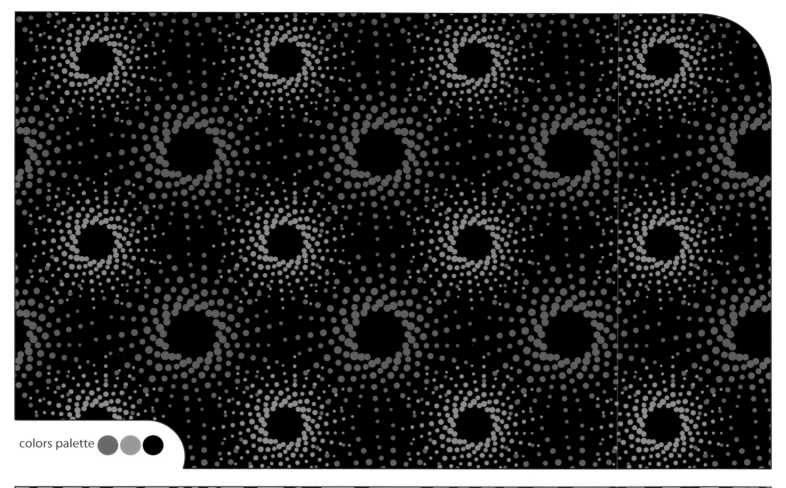

colors palette

colors palette

tp0087 / pattern size: 10,00 cm x 10,00 cm

pattern size: 21,00 cm x 30,00 cm / tp0088

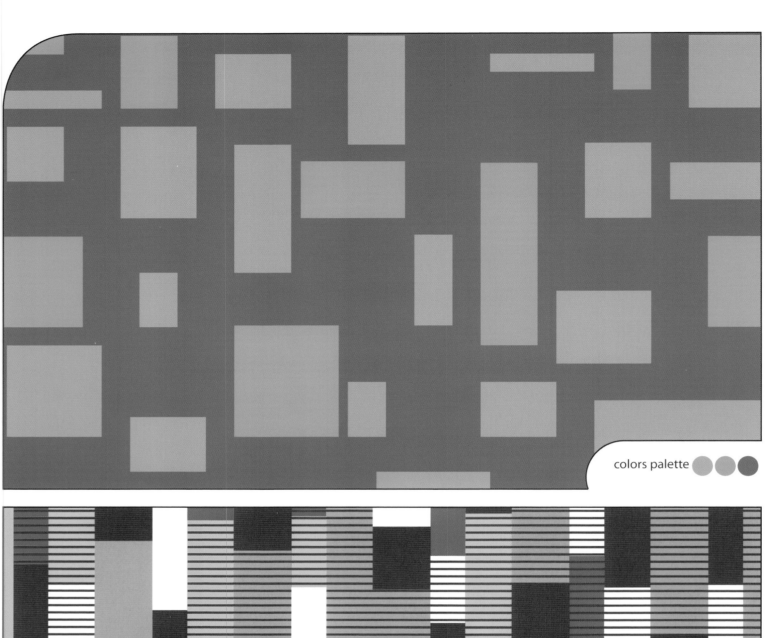

colors palette ●●●

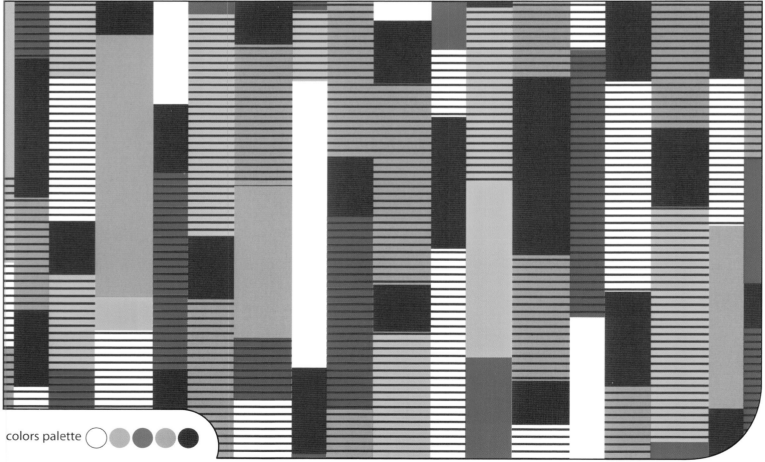

colors palette ○●●●●

tp0089 / pattern size: 21,50 cm x 29,50 cm

pattern size: 22,00 cm x 30,00 cm / tp0090

colors palette

pattern size: 21,50 cm x 29,50 cm / tp0091

colors palette ⚪⚫⚫⚫⚫

tp0092 / pattern size: 22,00 cm x 30,00 cm

colors palette

colors palette

colors palette

colors palette

tp0095 / pattern size: 15,40 cm x 21,00 cm

pattern size: 22,00 cm x 19,00 cm / tp0096

colors palette

pattern size: 22,00 cm x 30,00 cm / tp0097

colors palette

tp0098   / pattern size: 30,00 cm x 30,00 cm

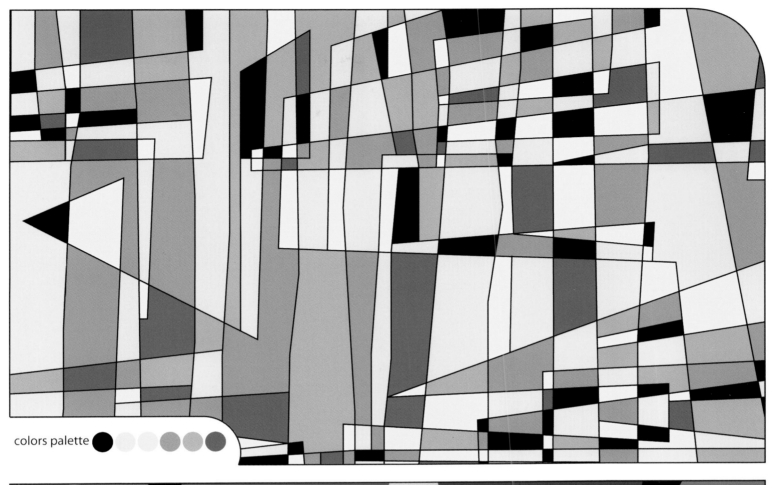

colors palette ●●●●●●●

colors palette ●●●●●●

tp0099 / pattern size: 24,00 cm x 30,00 cm

pattern size: 38,40 cm x 24,00 cm / tp0100

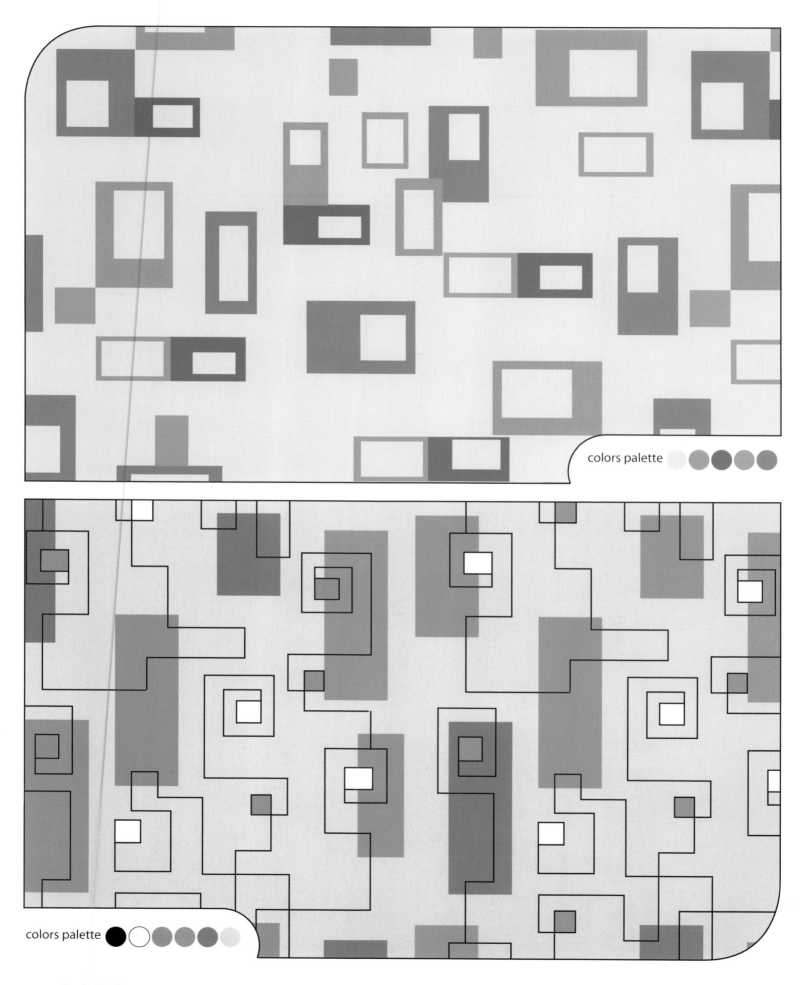

colors palette

colors palette

tp0101 / pattern size: 16,80 cm x 16,80 cm

pattern size: 22,40 cm x 22,40 cm / tp0102

colors palette

pattern size: 24,00 cm x 24,00 cm / tp0103

colors palette

tp0104 / pattern size: 44,00 cm x 38,00 cm

colors palette

colors palette

tp0105 / pattern size: 22,00 cm x 22,00 cm

pattern size: 41,60 cm x 26,00 cm / tp0106

FLORAL POP

It is a new season of geometric flowers. Not baroque or arabic but fresh modern shapes.

colors palette

colors palette

tp0107 / pattern size: 20,00 cm x 14,00 cm

pattern size: 18,00 cm x 18,00 cm / **tp0108**

colors palette

pattern size: 30,00 cm x 30,00 cm / tp0109

colors palette

tp0110 / pattern size: 26,00 cm x 26,00 cm

colors palette

colors palette

tp0111 / pattern size: 22,00 cm x 20,00 cm

pattern size: 29,40 cm x 22,40 cm / tp0112

colors palette

colors palette

tp0113 / pattern size: 25,00 cm x 25,00 cm

pattern size: 21,00 cm x 19,60 cm / tp0114

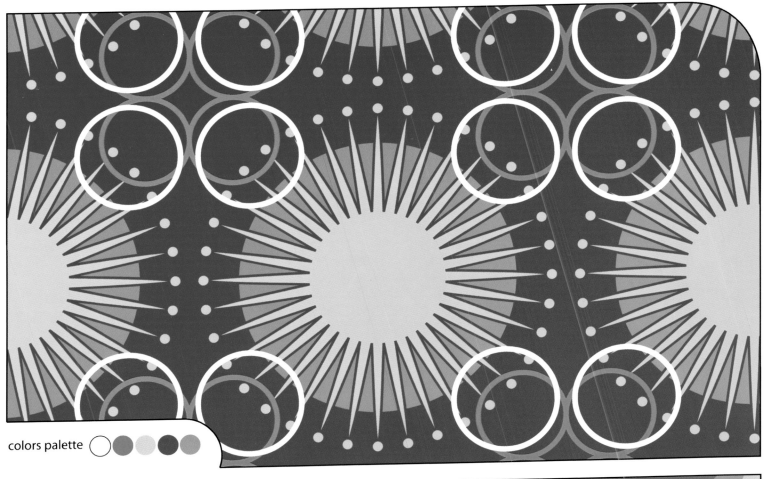

colors palette ⬭

colors palette ⬭

tp0115 / pattern size: 10,00 cm x 10,00 cm

pattern size: 16,80 cm x 26,60 cm / tp0116

colors palette

colors palette

tp0117 / pattern size: 22,00 cm x 22,00 cm

pattern size: 15,60 cm x 15,60 cm / tp0118

colors palette

pattern size: 28,00 cm x 28,00 cm / tp0119

colors palette

tp0120 / pattern size: 30,00 cm x 30,00 cm

colors palette

colors palette

tp0121 / pattern size: 24,00 cm x 24,00 cm

pattern size: 32,00 cm x 32,00 cm / tp0122

colors palette ⬤⬤⬤

colors palette ◯⬤⬤⬤⬤

tp0123 / pattern size: 5,04 cm x 5,04 cm

pattern size: 30,00 cm x 30,00 cm / tp0124

colors palette

colors palette

colors palette

colors palette

tp0127 / pattern size: 36,00 cm x 36,00 cm

pattern size: 24,00 cm x 32,00 cm / tp0128

colors palette

colors palette

tp0129 / pattern size: 29,00 cm x 21,00 cm

pattern size: 30,00 cm x 30,00 cm / tp0130

colors palette

colors palette

tp0131 / pattern size: 21,60 cm x 27,00 cm

pattern size: 19,20 cm x 19,20 cm / tp0132

colors palette

pattern size: 30,00 cm x 30,00 cm / tp0133

colors palette

tp0134   / pattern size: 30,00 cm x 30,00 cm

colors palette

pattern size: 22,00 cm x 22,00 cm / tp0135

colors palette

tp0136 / pattern size: 24,00 cm x 31,20 cm

colors palette

pattern size: 24,00 cm x 24,00 cm / tp0137

tp0138 / pattern size: 32,00 cm x 30,00 cm

pattern size: 24,00 cm x 24,00 cm / tp0139

colors palette

pattern size: 30,00 cm x 30,00 cm / tp0140

colors palette

tp0141 / pattern size: 24,00 cm x 24,00 cm

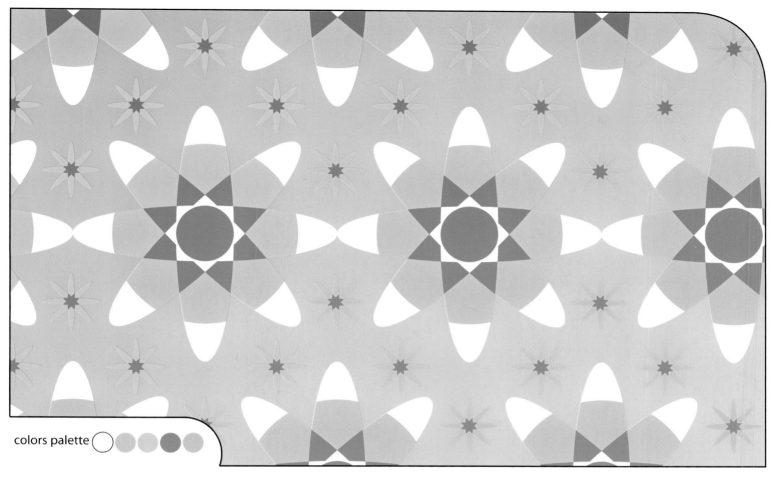

colors palette

colors palette

colors palette 〇 ⬤ ⬤ 〇 ⬤ ⬤

tp0144 / pattern size: 28,00 cm x 28,00 cm

colors palette ⬭ ⬤⬤⬤⬤⬤⬤⬤⬤⬤

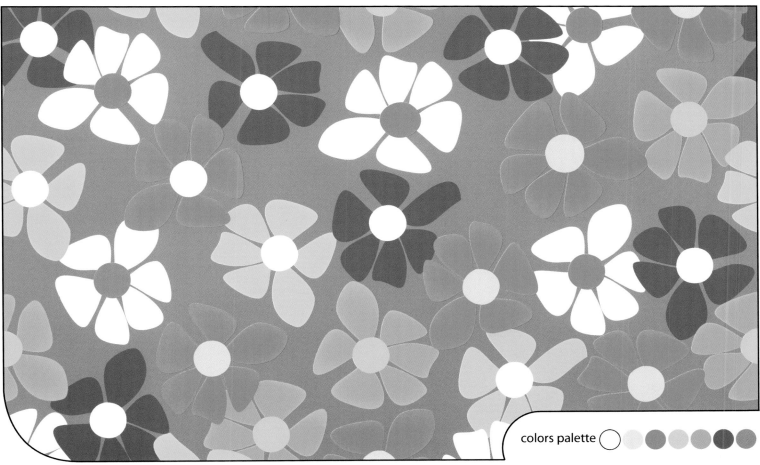

colors palette ⬭ ⬤⬤⬤⬤⬤⬤

tp0145 / pattern size: 24,00 cm x 24,00 cm

pattern size: 20,00 cm x 20,00 cm / **tp0146**

colors palette

tp0147 / pattern size: 24,00 cm x 24,00 cm

colors palette

colors palette

tp0148 / pattern size: 22,00 cm x 28,00 cm

pattern size: 30,00 cm x 30,00 cm / tp0149

colors palette ⚪ 🔵🔵🔵🔵 🔵

colors palette ⚪ 🔵🔵🔵🔵

tp0150 / pattern size: 20,00 cm x 20,00 cm

pattern size: 20,00 cm x 14,00 cm / **tp0151**

colors palette

pattern size: 20,00 cm x 14,50 cm / tp0152

colors palette

tp0153 / pattern size: 20,00 cm x 28,00 cm

colors palette ⚪⚫⚫⚫⚪⚫⚫⚫⚫⚫⚫⚪

pattern size: 20,00 cm x 26,10 cm / tp0154

colors palette

tp0155 / pattern size: 28,00 cm x 20,00 cm

colors palette

tp0156 / pattern size: 28,00 cm x 20,00 cm

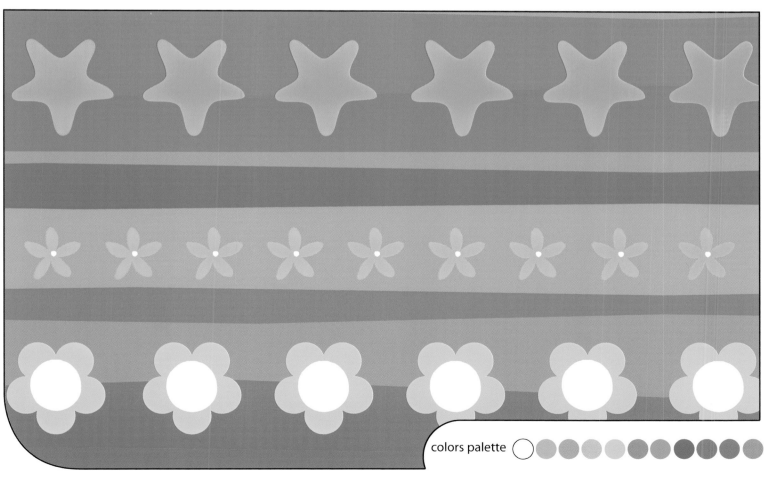

colors palette

pattern size: 28,00 cm x 20,00 cm / tp0157

SLICES OF POP

Slices of textures from the art of the sixties: Optical or Kinetic, Psychedelic or Pop Art itself.

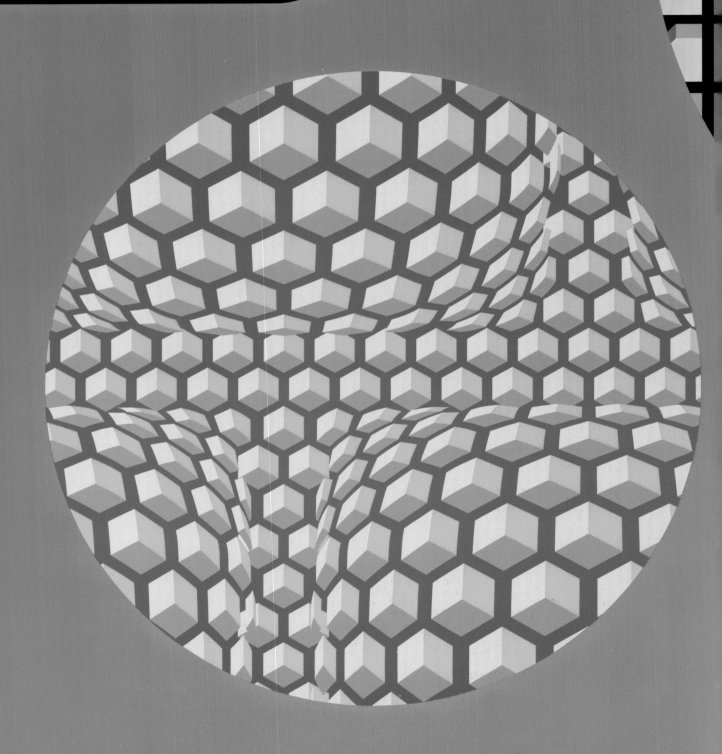

colors palette

colors palette

tp0158 / pattern size: 57,20 cm x 15,60 cm

pattern size: 30,00 cm x 24,00 cm / tp0159

colors palette

pattern size: 30,00 cm x 30,00 cm / tp0160

colors palette

tp0161 / pattern size: 20,00 cm x 20,00 cm

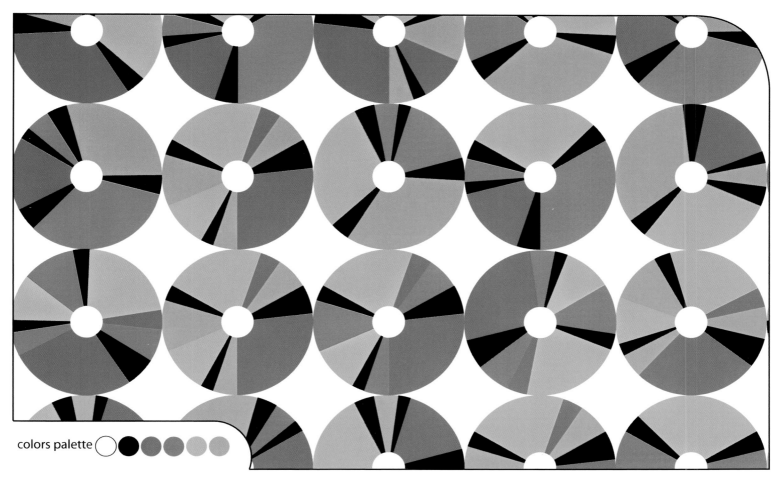

colors palette

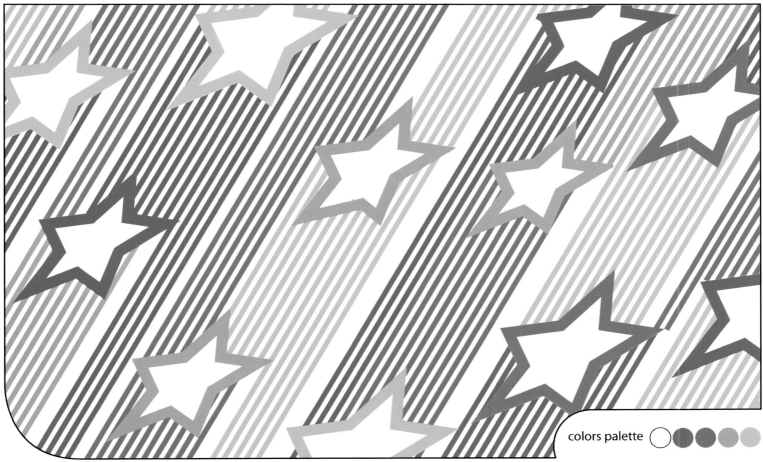

colors palette

tp0162 / pattern size: 20,00 cm x 20,00 cm

pattern size: 28,40 cm x 23,00 cm / tp0163

colors palette ●●●●●●●●

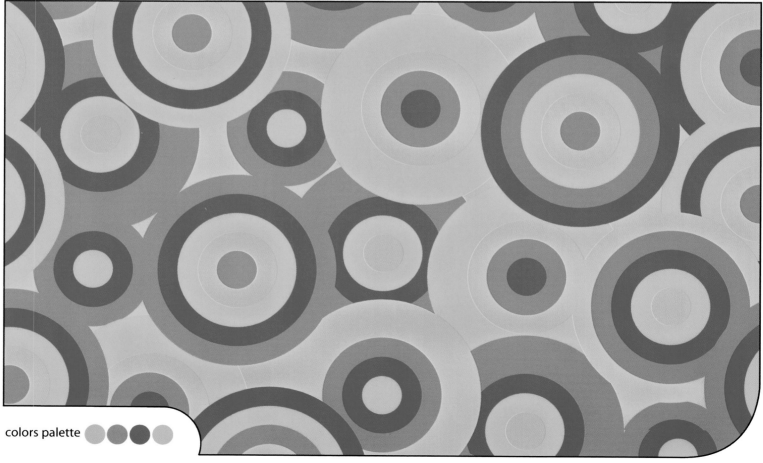

colors palette ●●●●●

tp0164 / pattern size: 30,00 cm x 30,00 cm

pattern size: 21,00 cm x 19,50 cm / tp0165

colors palette

colors palette

tp0166 / pattern size: 24,00 cm x 30,00 cm

pattern size: 20,00 cm x 14,00 cm / tp0167

colors palette

colors palette

tp0168 / pattern size: 40,00 cm x 36,80 cm

pattern size: 24,00 cm x 24,00 cm / tp0169

colors palette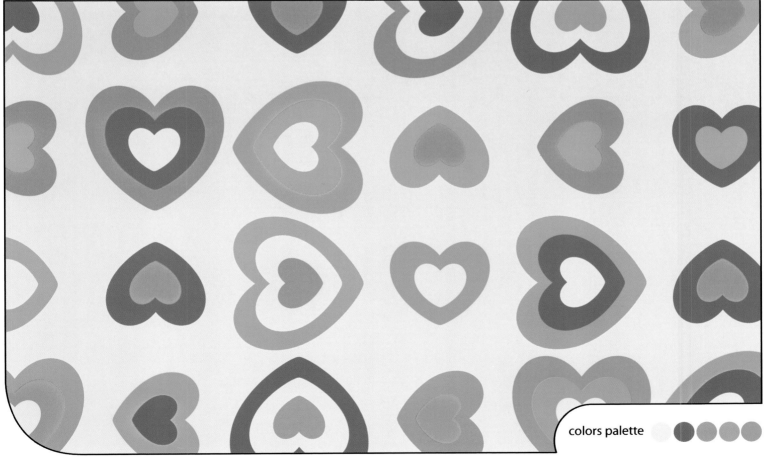

colors palette

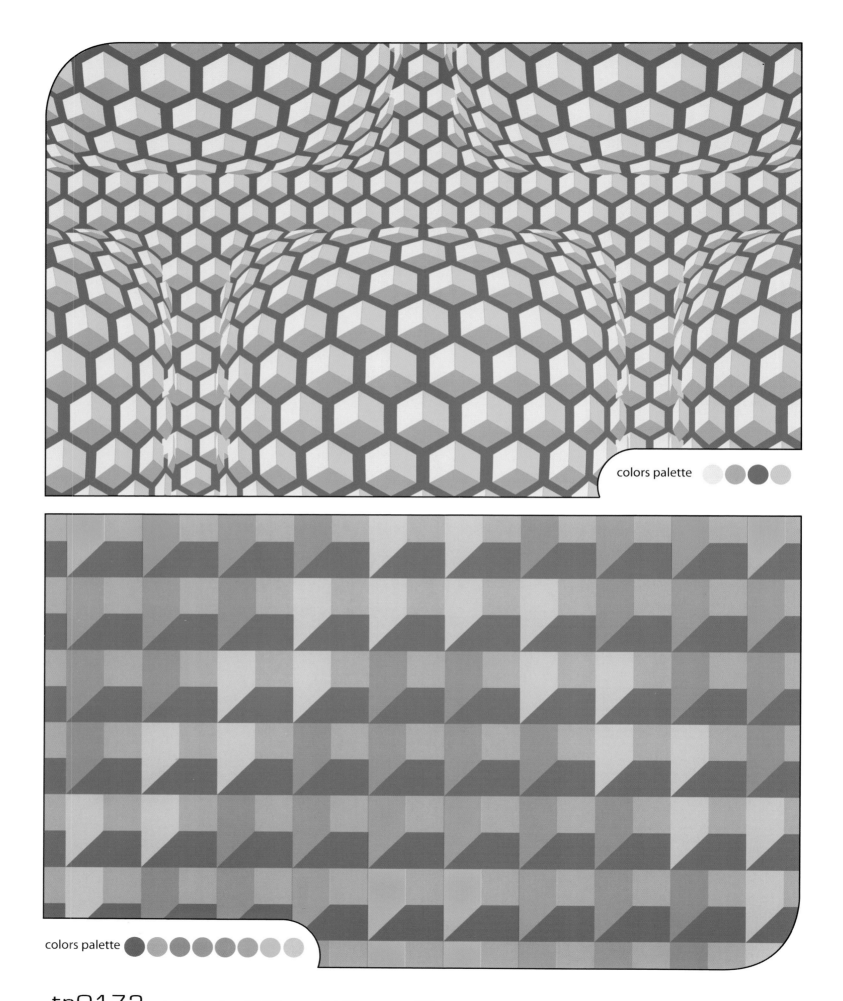

colors palette

colors palette

tp0172 / pattern size: 12,00 cm x 24,00 cm

pattern size: 26,00 cm x 26,00 cm / tp0173

colors palette

pattern size: 33,60 cm x 33,60 cm / tp0174

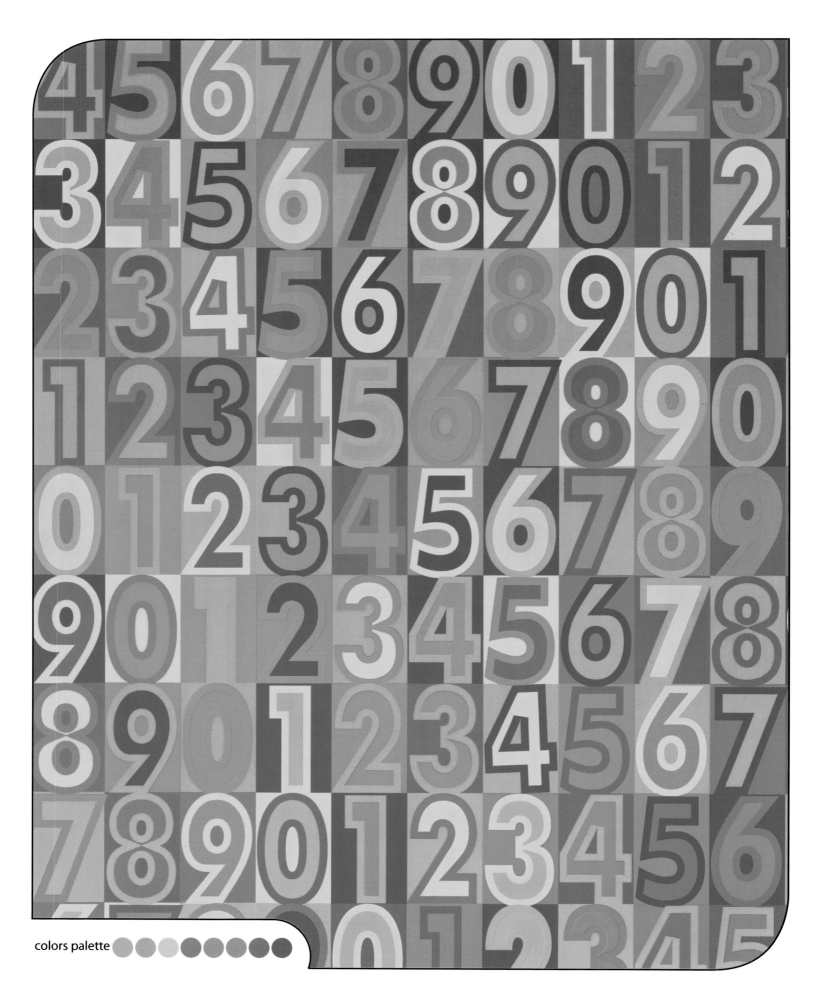

colors palette

tp0175 / pattern size: 20,00 cm x 30,00 cm

tp0176 / pattern size: 27,00 cm x 23,40 cm

pattern size: 27,00 cm x 23,40 cm / tp0177

colors palette

colors palette

tp0178 / pattern size: 24,00 cm x 18,00 cm

pattern size: 24,00 cm x 24,00 cm / **tp0179**

colors palette

colors palette

colors palette

colors palette

tp0182 / pattern size: 24,00 cm x 24,00 cm

pattern size: 24,00 cm x 24,00 cm / **tp0183**

colors palette

pattern size: 26,00 cm x 26,00 cm / tp0184

colors palette

tp0185 / pattern size: 25,00 cm x 27,00 cm

colors palette

colors palette

colors palette ○ ●

colors palette ○ ●

tp0188 / pattern size: 21,00 cm x 21,00 cm

pattern size: 20,00 cm x 30,00 cm / tp0189

colors palette ○ ●

pattern size: 20,00 cm x 20,00 cm / tp0190

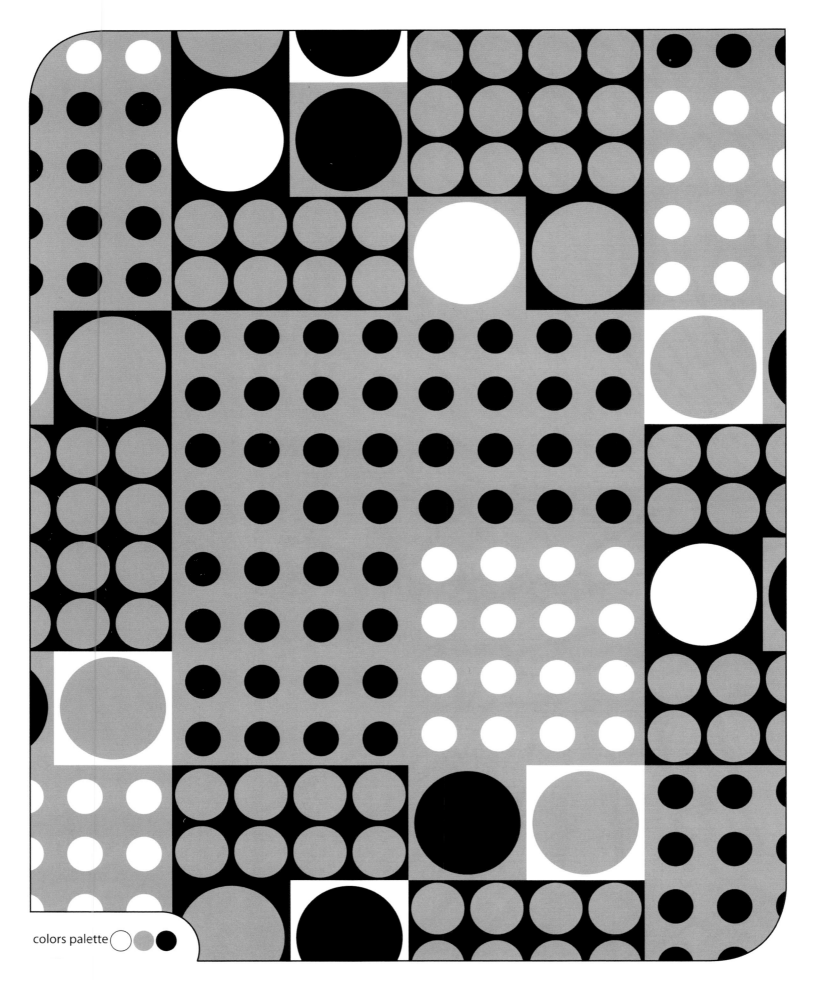

colors palette

tp0191 / pattern size: 25,00 cm x 25,00 cm

colors palette ○ ●

colors palette ○ ●

tp0192 / pattern size: 28,00 cm x 28,00 cm

pattern size: 21,675 cm x 21,675 cm / tp0193

tp0194 / pattern size: 36,00 cm x 36,00 cm

colors palette ○ ●

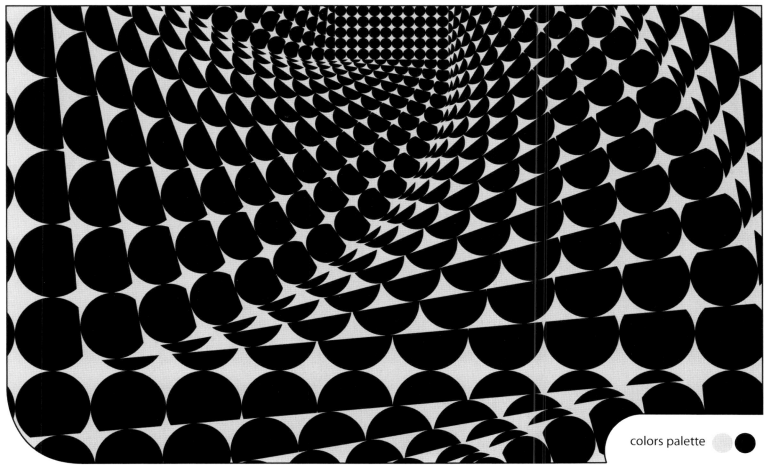

colors palette ○ ●

tp0195 / pattern size: 20,00 cm x 20,00 cm

pattern size: 20,00 cm x 20,00 cm / tp0196

colors palette ⚪⚫

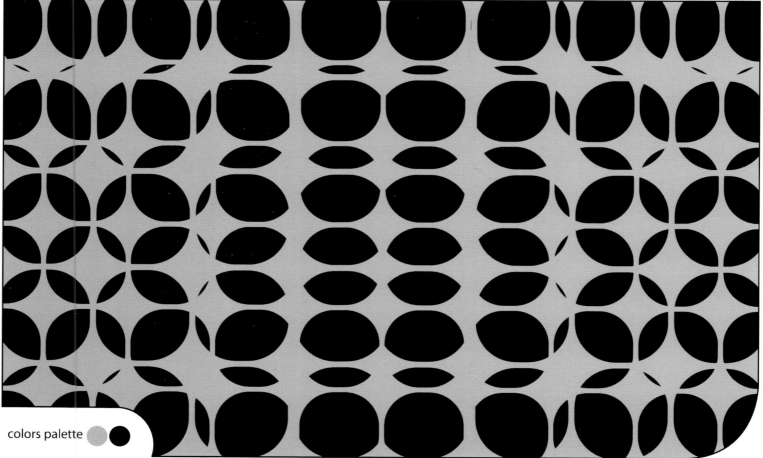

colors palette 🔘⚫

tp0197 / pattern size: 15,40 cm x 15,40 cm

pattern size: 17,92 cm x 17,92 cm / **tp0198**

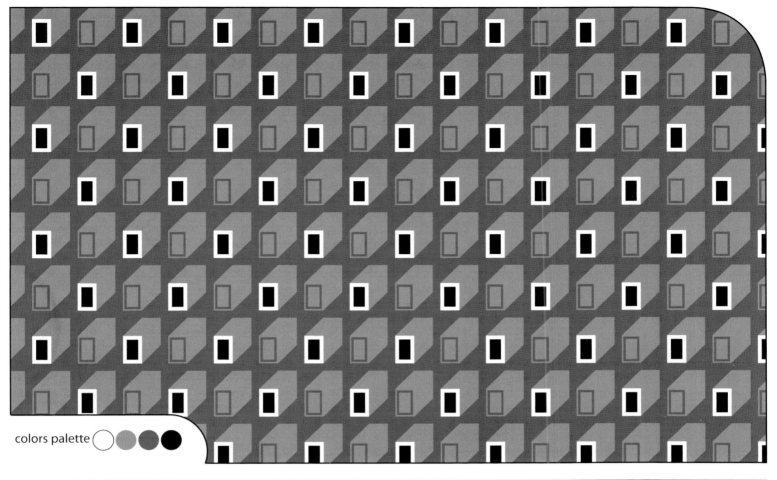

colors palette ◯ ◉ ◉ ●

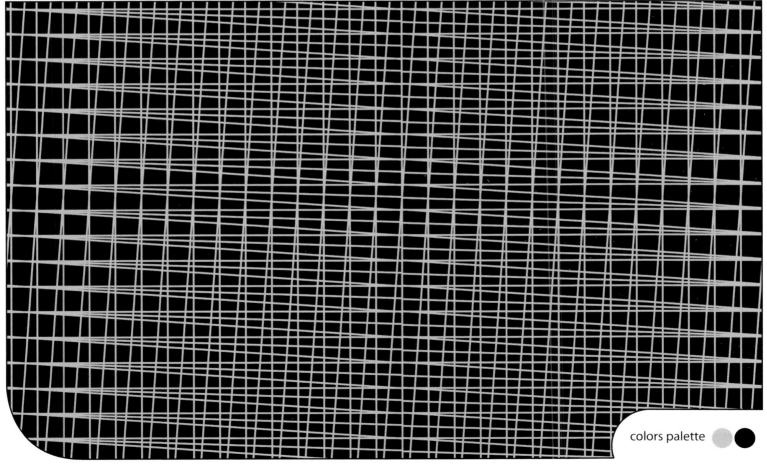

colors palette ◉ ●

tp0199 / pattern size: 12,00 cm x 14,50 cm

pattern size: 20,00 cm x 20,00 cm / tp0200

Published by
VINCENZO SGUERA

Via Provinciale , 68
24022 Alzano Lombardo
Bergamo (Italy)
Phone: (0039) 035515851

e-mail:
info@vincenzosguera.com

ARKIVIA
Books for Style
published by Vincenzo Sguera